Advance Praise

At times of great loss, it is hard to find a true companion, one who will understand your deep sorrow and not try to get you to move on. Patricia McKernon Runkle is that worthy companion. While recounting in searing detail her response to the loss of her brother, she shines the light of her attention on the poems of Emily Dickinson, whom she chooses as her own fierce companion, and they bloom for us as never before. Most powerful of all, she shares her own diamond-like work—finely wrought prose interwoven with her own spare, honest, kind, and deeply wise poetry. In *Grief's Compass*, she creates a space in which readers can visit their own grieving and explore the way stations she has found. This book is a sanctuary, a refuge. There is medicine in these pages.

— Susan Deborah (Sam) King
Poet, teacher, retreat leader, consultant

Patricia McKernon Runkle's unfailing devotion to the ache of truth taps the universality of loss in lines like this—"Where was the Gardener in his life, at his death?" And this—"Where does the eye want to look?" And then—"Do parts of the self, like tendrils, latch on to truths until finally the whole self heaves into a new center?" Poetry by Emily Dickinson laces through Runkle's story without distracting from her own stunning voice. Slim and spare, *Grief's Compass* is a treasure to hold close.

— Julie Maloney
Founder/Director
Women Reading Aloud

Grief's Compass asks us to step into the unknown and be made new. In this beautiful story, Runkle helps us feel the struggle between sorrow and re-emergence as she delicately searches for wholeness in the midst of grief.

Along the way, she reminds us to help children navigate the chaos that grief creates and the self-discovery that awaits on the horizon.

— Joseph M. Primo, M.Div.
Chief Executive Officer, Good Grief, Inc.
Children's Grief Support Centers

This story has the feel of a physical touch, of one griever reaching out to another with a clear message: you are not alone. Patricia offers grievers tangible hope—not merely a wish that things will get better—and meaningful points on a compass to navigate and gradually return to normalcy, comfort, and inner peace.

— Judith A. Pedersen, MSW
Founder and Executive Director
Hearts of Hope Foundation, Inc.

Patricia McKernon Runkle's *Grief's Compass* is a luminous journey through the landscape of grief. Patricia's vivid collage—of memoir, journal, and poetry—dances with Emily Dickinson, who becomes a fearless muse helping Patricia navigate the tragic death of her brother. Patricia does not reduce grief to a neat Kübler-Ross process, nor does she offer advice. She embraces, as Emily did, the abyss: "Before me was a challenge: to give up wanting to know. Beyond that challenge was another: to give up assuming that I could know." So intimate and honest is this work, so vivid and insightful the writing, that, as a reader, you will feel that Patricia's voice is your voice; her pain, yours; her triumphs, yours. *Grief's Compass* proves what Dickinson wrote: "'Nothing' is the force that renovates the world." More than being a stellar addition to the treasury of works about Dickinson, this book is "a hand reaching for yours."

— Susanna Rich, Ph.D.
Poet and Distinguished Professor
Kean University
Union, New Jersey

GRIEF'S COMPASS

Walking the Wilderness with Emily Dickinson

GRIEF'S COMPASS

Walking the Wilderness with Emily Dickinson

Patricia McKernon Runkle

Apprentice House
Loyola University Maryland
Baltimore, Maryland

Six of the author's poems were published previously in the following journals: "After" in *Peregrine* (2012), "Blue" in *Salamander* (2011), "Grief" in *Grey Sparrow* (2012), "In the Basilica" in *Eclipse* (2013), "In the Darkness" in *decomP* (2011), "The Great Benevolence" in *Quiddity* (2012).

First Edition
Printed in the United States of America

Casebound ISBN: 978-1-62720-159-9
Paperback ISBN: 978-1-62720-160-5
E-book ISBN: 978-1-62720-161-2

Design by Olivia Airhart
Author photo by Dee Tamayo
Published by Apprentice House

Apprentice House
Loyola University Maryland
4501 N. Charles Street
Baltimore, MD 21210
410.617.5265 • 410.617.2198 (fax)
www.apprenticehouse.com
info@apprenticehouse.com

For my brother Bill
1960 – 2004

Contents

Foreword

PICKING UP THE COMPASS

A Wilderness of Size

Emily Dickinson

On a gray day deep in winter, my brother Bill died . . . by suicide. I always want to pause before I say that word. It's a frozen stream I step across gingerly. Bill was 43. He left a wife, five children, and a wake of stunned survivors.

~

There is a pain – so utter –
It swallows substance up –

These are the words that spoke to me after my brother died. They are the opening lines of a poem by Emily Dickinson. I had tracked it down years earlier after reading Joyce Carol Oates's opinion that it must be one of the most terrifying poems ever written. When I first encountered it, its meaning was impenetrable, partly because of the language. A pain so intense—why call it *utter*? It swallows *substance*—what sort of substance was she talking about?

Yet as I reread the poem after my brother's death, it began to take on meaning. Its opening lines captured the sense of being devoured. The message was clear: extreme pain is all-consuming.

Then covers the Abyss with Trance –
So Memory can step
Around – across – upon it –
As One within a Swoon –
Goes safely –

Numbness, Dickinson implied, is a form of protection for a shocked mind. It's a rickety plank set over a well to prevent a person from falling in. Not that she said this in so many words. She didn't use the word *well*, but I saw one. She didn't say the cover was rickety, but I felt it was. She didn't say *grief*; she said *pain*. To the Rorschach image of the poem, I brought my grief and my imagination.

I walked the plank with her and listened as she cautioned not to peek over

where an open eye –
Would drop Him – Bone by Bone.

If you could see, she said, if you could feel all the pain at once, you'd be shattered. You'd be a loose collection of bones—your bones—falling down a bottomless well.

Horrifying.

Now I knew she was someone I could trust.

~

"The Wilderness is new – to you. Master, let me lead you." Dickinson wrote these words to her friend and literary mentor shortly after his wife died, inviting him to trust her intimate knowledge of grief's landscape. I took her for my guide and companion as well. Whichever way I turned, she'd walked there—with her ragged, barefoot heart, as she once called it—and left a flag, a pile of rocks, a carving in a tree trunk. She didn't say grief goes in stages. That matched my experience. There were no stages. There were states of mind and turning points.

I began to picture a compass, an image that had the power to help me know where I stood. It had four cardinal points: loss, story, memory, and healing. These points were not immediately obvious; they emerged gradually as I began to get my bearings. South was the blown-apart, numbed-out state of shock I felt after my brother's death. This I took from the common saying "Things went south." East, where the sun rises, was the place for my attempts at narrative. Immediately afterward and long into the future, I needed a story that would shine a light on my experience. Then there were the glowing memories that both comforted and haunted me. These I thought of as West because, at the end of the day, memories of my brother were all I had, and because remembering is kin to dreaming. North represented moments of insight. Like the earth's magnetic pole, intuitions gave me a bearing and helped me move forward.

With the compass metaphor in mind and Dickinson's poems and letters in hand, I began to chart a path through my wilderness.

In *Grief's Compass*, the path includes stories, journal entries, and poems of mine mixed in with Dickinson's writing. This makes for many writing styles and voices. The book is itself a wilderness, a witness to the complexity of grief. Journal entries and poems in the chapter called South, for example, are fragmented, disjointed—the way shock feels. Not all of my story is told there because, when grief was fresh, I had no coherent narrative; South was the place of nothing, nowhere. Other chapters walk the wilderness in their own ways. East, like a good story, is linear and more organized. West, like memory, dissolves time and flows. North, like intuition, explores, unifies, and leads to turning points.

As time went on, North became the most important point on my compass. In fact, it takes up three chapters in this book. Why? On the great magnet of the earth, North is the point that matters. Ships and planes, explorers and wanderers, geese and sea turtles all find their way by it. North is the soul's magnetic pole. It furthers healing. In some inexplicable way, it is healing itself.

~

When you dig to the root of *healing*, you find that this word has to do with health, wholeness, even holiness. In my experience, all of this is true. The ragged work of grief may feel like madness. But, as Dickinson said, "Much Madness is divinest Sense – / To a discerning Eye –."

Grief is a holy madness. It is not a puzzle to be solved, a problem to be overcome, or a situation to be managed. It is a wilderness we wander in search of the sacred—an absent other, a missing self. No one can take this wilderness from us, and no one should. You who grieve, stay away from people who want you to get over it fast. They don't know that the work you're doing is holy.

SOUTH

Loss

1

WHAT HAPPENED

I, and Silence, some strange Race
Wrecked, solitary, here –

Emily Dickinson

Now I know.

When someone tells the date of a death, pay attention. It is a roadside shrine. Like a mound of stones or a city of candles, it marks a date you must pass year after year.

On this site, lives and dreams were crushed.

My brother Bill ended his life on February 4, 2004. This much I can say. Other facts I can't say, either because I don't know them or they're not my story to tell. I don't know (can't know) all the events that led to his suicide, when he began seriously to consider the plan, or how he knew—*knew*—that February 4 was the day. These are matters he kept so private that no one sensed how close to death he was.

Other matters deserve to remain private. How his wife and children survived the wake, the funeral, and their afterlife, as one person called it. Certain conversations, pointed questions, regrets. In fact, anything from anyone else's perspective but my own is off this map.

The real subject of this story is grief itself: the huge bewilderness of it. My grief began the moment I answered my cell phone. I was driving my younger daughter home from school when my sister called and asked, "Where are you?" When I answered, "Driving home, nearly there," she said she had important news about Bill and she'd call me back in five minutes.

A mercy, those last five minutes of normal.

~

Normal is what you have before you lose it.

My sister told me, in words I will not repeat for privacy's sake, that Bill was dead and how he died. I called out her name—not his—sharply, as if to say *How dare you say that!* This was my introduction to the madness, the irrationality of grief. How we fend off, throw off bad news. The heavier it is, the harder we fling it away.

I knew that my brother was troubled and had been unstable for months. In the last phone conversation we had, he'd said, again and again, "I feel confused. I just feel *so* confused."

But . . . suicide?

I began to cry, a full-body wail that sent my daughter flying upstairs. I found her later, after the call, huddled under her desk. This was my first glimpse of the effect this death was to have on the children of the family.

If this story were a news article, I would catalog the events of the next five days. Unfortunately, it is reality, and reality comes and goes. It occurs in moments, units of meaning that become memories. Or they fade away. The fact is, I don't remember everything. As I discovered, a numbness sets in—"an Element of Blank," Dickinson called it—that shields the mind and heart from the intensity of pain.

Of course, I immediately told my daughter that her uncle had died, though I didn't use the word *suicide* just then. Of course, I made a flock of phone calls. Of course, my husband and I soon explained to both of our children the truth of the situation.

Of course, I felt angry. I say *of course* now, but at the time this feeling surprised me. After the first flood of shock and weeping, I felt a wave of anger. How could he do this? What about his children? His wife? His responsibilities? How could he just . . . die?

These questions surfaced again in a phone call to my sister-in-law, Bill's—widow?—another impossibility. They could not be answered. They stuck on the mind like burrs. Her assessment sufficed: "His pain swallowed him." To this day, it is the best way I know to describe my brother's death. He did not survive the pain so utter.

Bill's death violates all sense of order.

To put these words on a page is to set them down, one after another, the way we walk: first one foot, then the other, as if there were a journey and a destination, a place we hoped to get to.

If there was such a place, Bill did not find it. I could say he lost his footing, but that would not begin to convey the bleakness of his despair or the rawness of our wound.

THREE SCENES

▪ ▪ ▪

At our mother's kitchen table

▪ ▪ ▪

My sister says softly, "I wish I could have held him."
She opens her arms, as if enfolding him.
"I wish I could have held him and told him, 'Your life is worth saving'."
Her tears.

▪ ▪ ▪

Before the wake, the viewing

▪ ▪ ▪

His mother wants an open casket. His wife, closed.
So, a private viewing two hours before the wake.
Half a dozen of us, in silence.
Bill's perfect stillness.
My shaking.

Why they call it a viewing: they don't want to call it a stabbing, a bleeding, a blinding.

▪ ▪ ▪

At the funeral

▪ ▪ ▪

The choir has sung us into the church with the most mournful singing I have ever heard. We, the survivors, are seated in the front pew waiting for Mass to begin.

My sister whispers to me, "She wants to sing the Ave Maria."

I'm astounded. "How can she possibly *do* that?"

A lifelong singer, our mother had sung this piece at our father's funeral, two months earlier. She had stood, solid and composed, and offered it for him. "He always loved that one," she said. But now? Today? At *this* funeral?

"We can't let her do it alone," my sister whispers back. "We have to go up there with her—hold her hands or something."

I think: *No way. I cannot do this. I will absolutely blubber. I will sink to my knees. I will picture Bill praying the rosary the day before he died, and I will not make it through.*

But, in one of those epiphanies that sometimes actually happen in church, a stillness steals over me. In the quiet, a thought comes, a thought so fully formed and authoritative it does not seem like my own. *You are not the star*, it says. *<u>You</u> are not the star.*

I look around. I see my sister-in-law, Bill's wife; my mother, Bill's mother; my nieces and nephews, Bill's children; my sister and brothers, Bill's family; my own family. This is everyone's day, everyone's hour; it's not just about me and my feelings. If my mother has the strength to stand up and sing the Ave Maria, then, by God, it's my job to help her do it.

And so, when the organist begins the intro and my mother leaves the pew, my sister and I step out with her and walk to the front of the church. She sings steadily, all the way through; poised, honoring her faith. As she sings, my sister takes her right hand and I take her left. Instinctively, we lift our outer hands upward. The three of us become a tableau, a living sculpture: a mother flanked by her daughters, three women at the foot of a cross.

AFTER

the blank page
    is here   again
the page is
          the white
    page   is black
      the pencil is
a pen
  the finger a foot
              the lamp is dark
    the here is there
        the then is now   the
why is   no
      the know is   how?

The utter silence of raw grief. I did not, could not, chronicle that time.

It was a black cave I banged around in. It was white tundra I trudged over. It was a chasm I whistled down. It was an echo chamber. It was dead space. I forgot things. I remembered things. I cried at stoplights. I sat on the floor—pet the dog, pet the dog, pet the dog. Food was nothing. Time was nothing. Nothing was everything. Everything was nothing.

N
W
E
S

Grief is a Mouse –
And chooses Wainscot in the Breast
For His shy House –
And baffles quest –

Grief is a Thief – quick startled –
Pricks His Ear – report to hear
Of that Vast Dark –
That swept His Being – back –

Grief is a Juggler – boldest at the Play –
Lest if He flinch – the eye that way
Pounce on His Bruises – One – say – or Three –
Grief is a Gourmand – spare His luxury –

Best Grief is Tongueless – before He'll tell –
Burn Him in the Public square –
His Ashes – will
Possibly – if they refuse – How then know –
Since a Rack couldn't coax a syllable – now

Emily Dickinson

Grief is a mouse, Dickinson tells us. Elusive, it scuttles in and out of the hole it gnaws in the heart's façade.

Then, too, grief is a thief. Jumpy. On the alert for telltale news of his theft. There he goes, thumping his bag of stolen goods over his shoulder, stealthy as death. Yet, unlike the mouse, this thief has no protection. Grief itself is swept backward into immense darkness.

Catch this, she says: grief is a juggler. See his third ball? It's in the air, he can't hold it. It's not in his hands, yet he has it. He's a grieving person, who has and does not have his loved one. He works courageously at the edge of chaos and injury.

Now he's a gourmand, a lover of fine foods. What's on the menu? Memory, tears, regret, despair—the poor soul has nothing. Why? Loss is an abundance of absence. But if, in grieving, he dines on loss alone, what will sustain him? How can he live, and why should he?

In the end, Dickinson says, grief is mute. It has no word for itself. She shows him from three angles at once, like a figure in a cubist painting. He might tell, so burn him. Even his ashes could reveal the story. Then again, they might not; if not, we'll never know the truth of his suffering. Might tell, can't tell, won't tell—three ways of not talking. What's best about this? Nothing, really. It's just the clearest way to explain that grief cannot explain itself. It has no tongue.

EAST

Story

2

BUT . . . WHAT HAPPENED?

And grateful that a thing
So terrible – had been endured –
I told my Soul to sing –

Emily Dickinson

I knew what happened. But . . . what *happened*?

If only I had a story—a meaningful narrative, not just facts—I could see by its light. I could estimate the size of the loss and distance myself from it. I could have the experience, not be it. My problem was, I had two ways to tell what happened, and neither was satisfactory. I could not understand it. I could describe my brother's death, but I could not make sense of it.

~

A 3-D cube flips in and out of the page.

Lifts up to the right or shoots down to the left.

Bill's death flips around, like the cube. It won't settle down. And I can't see both views at once.

Is a story a story if it can't be understood?

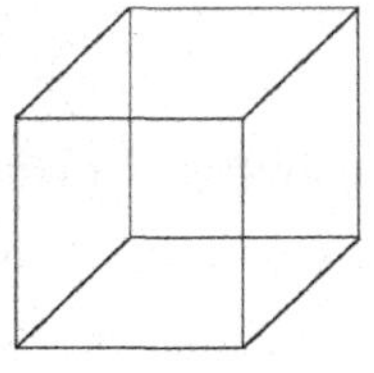

Bill was the one I rarely worried about. He was outgoing, fun, charismatic. You could meet him and in five minutes feel you had a friend. He didn't wait for you to like him; he liked you first.

He was the first to say he loved me. We were not a demonstrative family, but he melted barriers. He had that ability; we had that bond. An example: We were in the car one night. I was driving, he was in the passenger seat. Both in our twenties, we were having a long discussion on Life, The Universe, Everything. Street lamps flickered past. After a long pause, he said, "You know what?" Slowly, deliberately, "I love you."

Even in childhood, Bill stood out. He got a paper route and learned the names of everyone in our neighborhood. He saved his money, bought a lawn mower, and started a mowing business. In college, he majored in economics and then became a banker—a person who puts money and people together. He had such a combination of innate talent and hard work that eventually he became the general manager of one of the large downtown banks in New Haven.

Is this a success story? It is. Bill was the most prominent member of our family. But Bill had interior struggles; few people outside the family knew. He had had a serious case of depression for many years. He'd become so adept at hiding his troubles that, when he began to spin out of control, not even those closest to him knew he was suicidal.

We did know that Bill was unbalanced, especially in the months after our father died. The last time we got together, at Christmas, he sat alone on a couch, staring mutely into space. We did not know he was fighting: *must live / must die / must live / must die.*

On February 4, 2004, *must die* won.

His wake was huge. People stood outside in the cold for 45 minutes, only to wait another 45 minutes inside, just to walk up to his wife and say things like these: "I got my promotion because of him." "He helped my daughter get her wish from the Make-A-Wish

Foundation." "He tutored my cousin's friend." "He convinced me to go back to school." "He helped me start my business." "He was one of the kindest people I knew."

After Bill's funeral, one of our brothers said he'd lost his best friend. Our mother, who had lost her husband two months earlier, now lost a beloved son. She also lost a daughter-in-law and five grandchildren. Within six months of the funeral, they did what was right for them; they moved back to my sister-in-law's hometown. I lost a brother, a friend, and a way of trusting. For a time, I lost my mind—the ability to understand something by thinking about it. Each member of the family lost someone or something precious. In this, we were now bonded to every other mourner.

When I talked one day with a friend whose family had also lived through a suicide, she said, "I died. What I have now is an afterlife." My sister-in-law said, "The whole house burned down." I said, "I lost my mind." Why do we need these outsize metaphors? Because suicide can do that much damage. It is a death like no other because it is chosen. It is bigger and deeper, more painful and vexing than anyone can possibly say. Nothing is the same afterward.

Yet any significant death can do this much damage. A friend of mine was 26 when her mother died. As she told me the story, we were sitting at a table covered by a mat that could fold up in half. "It's like this," she said. "There's this part of your life"—sweeping up to the midline—"and then there's the rest of it"—sweeping past the line to the edge of the table.

Emily Dickinson had her version of this dividing line. In a poem that begins "We grow accustomed to the Dark – / When Light is put away –," she tells us that we can learn to see, but our vision is dark-adapted and our gait is off.

Either the Darkness alters –
Or something in the sight
Adjusts itself to Midnight –
And Life steps almost straight.

My mind staggered. I could describe Bill's suicide. I could say it happened over time. His descent was long, and slow at first. In the end, everything that could go wrong did go wrong, and everyone had reasons not to see. But to describe it is not to understand it.

A meaningful event is something we can draw a shape around—give it boundaries or contours against a larger background. When someone dies in military service, for example, we call that person a patriot. When someone dies trying to save someone else, we call that person a hero. But when someone dies after a long or painful illness, we begin to have trouble explaining. The person did not deserve to die in this way, at this time; he should have lived. Accidents are even harder to accept, especially when the person is young. The background evaporates; the boundaries melt. *This is unfair, this is wrong*, we think.

I had no way to shape this unfair, wrong thing. My brother's death was not an accident, but it was like an accident. It wasn't an illness, but it resulted from illness—"as if / His Mind were going blind –." Dickinson wrote this line in a poem dealing explicitly with suicide. At the end of the poem, a staggering, helpless man has "Caressed a Trigger absently / And wandered out of Life –." How correct these words all seemed. The beguiling, creepy *caressed*. The aimless *wander*. The deadly *absent*. The sense of something out of control, yet controlling the man.

Was my brother responsible for his death? Yes, he caused himself to die. But he, the person we knew, did not choose it; "he" was not "himself." His body was healthy, but his mind was a train, wrecking.

Lines from another Dickinson poem captured the two sides of this story.

Never Bud from a stem
Stepped with so gay a Foot
Never a Worm so confident
Bored at so brave a Root

Yes, Bill's death was self-inflicted, but he inherited his depression. It was there at the root. Every day he got up and fought his worm, until the day he didn't. Where was the Gardener in his life, at his death?

FLYBY

We love to hear about angels who do their jobs—
    stifle ravenous lions, rescue innocent babies.
But what about the ones who don't show up?
    Who don't bear tidings of comfort or joy.
    Who don't push back as someone makes his final descent.
    Who don't whisper, "Think of your children."

We like to believe an angel will appear and talk us out of some terrible deed.
Clarence did that for George Bailey, who was about to leap off a bridge.
    (Not really. That was a movie.)
    (Jimmy Stewart was safe as pie, snug as toast.)
But remember? Clarence saves George by getting George
    to save *him* (a wicked clever plan) and then goes on
    to show George how his good deeds have saved the town.
See the cameraman smiling as the bell tinkles and Clarence gets his wings?
The imagination flies at 24 frames per second.

The movie we made takes place after nearly 20 years of depression.
George's wife is about to leave him and take the children far away.
George has two doctors and three medications.
The doctors (who don't consult each other) are changing his meds and dosages.
George is in the danger place, the no-fly zone.

Right about this time, George's father dies, and George
    (who, being human, has no wings)
    (and who, being human, is feeling wobbly)
one day tells his wife
    this is where the insurance papers are,
    this is where the tax records are.

Soon after that, George goes to a bridge and stares into the water.
Mr. Potter stops by.
    "Is this a good way to kill myself?" George asks.
    "Oh yes," Mr. Potter says, "it works quite well. Many people do it this way."

The next day, George goes back to the bridge.
Clarence is not there to show him how he gave his town wings.
Scene deleted: struggling children who now have mentors.
Scene deleted: gravely ill children granted their fondest wish.
Scene deleted: people who went on in school because George believed in them.
Scene deleted: people who ran their own business because George gave them a loan.
Scene deleted: George's five children, who love him and need him.

And so, in our movie, George
(for whom people are praying)

George
(who is seen praying the rosary
the day before he dies)

George
(for whom no one shows up, not even
the cameraman)

George

jumps

Why wasn't my brother saved? Where was his Clarence? I didn't expect a literal angel. I don't believe in literal angels. Yet I come from people who do, and somewhere, deep in my child-mind, I wanted a rescue. In my rational mind, I knew the truth: people we love are not saved just because we love them. Yet this hard, spiky truth rubbed my skin off. In my cockeyed rage and horror, I wanted a simple God. A small God. A God I could understand and manage.

I wanted a God who catches falling sparrows. Dickinson's question haunted me: ". . . and what indeed is Earth but a Nest, from whose rim we are all falling?" These lines of hers spoke my mind:

Of Course – I prayed –
And did God Care?
He cared as much as on the Air
A Bird – had stamped her foot –
And cried "Give Me" –

~

Here's Bill flailing his wings, stamping the air. "Help! Helpp!! Hellllppp!!!"

A falling sparrow, an absent hand. This story matches the facts . . . but doesn't satisfy.

A desperate person, a saving God. This story is told in church . . . but doesn't match the facts.

How could a person of such goodness and faith die so utterly alone? The question bedevils me.

I needed a story big enough and loving enough to hold my horror. The senior minister at my church had such a story, but I couldn't accept it then. When I blurted out, in my shocked, child-mind naiveté, "Where were my brother's keepers?" he answered simply and quietly, "Weeping beside him."

The only story I could tell was *shattered*, as when a crystal vase falls to the floor.

> If a precious life shatters in solitude, does God's ear hear?
>
> If God's ear does not hear, why did Bill pray? Why did I pray?
>
> If I can hear the sound of weeping, why can't God?
>
> If God heard and yet Bill died, what does this mean?
>
> Which is worse: If God's ear does not hear? Or if it does?

~

With my rational mind, I could not grasp what was happening to me or make my way through it. Of course not. If all of being is a mountain, rationality is a tiny robot scanning it. On the surface. In the dark. With a flashlight.

> How can you use part of yourself to understand what's happening to all of yourself?

I needed everything, my whole self, to pull through grief: dreams, intuitions, conversations, poems, hope, imagination, even my ignorance. Especially my ignorance. I needed to allow mystery, to not-know all the answers. Not know why things hadn't happened differently. Not know whether, or how, my family and I would heal. Not know what would come next. Not know when the pain would end. Not know the inner and outer edges of my own self.

My children, too, needed to use all their resources to work through this loss. I tell the following story about my younger daughter, with her permission. I tell it to remind us all to pay attention to the children. They know what's happening. They need to tell their stories. They ask the big questions. And they have their own ability to heal, their North.

Just after we came home from the funeral, I was dropping off my daughter at school. She was 10 years old. "Mom," she said slowly, "I had the weirdest dream." With one hand on the car door handle, ready to bolt, she told me her dream. "Wow," I said quietly, when she had finished, "and . . . it feels weird to you." She nodded and began to open the door. "You know," I added, "it seems to me this is a story you're telling yourself. It can help you." But she shook her head. "No. It wasn't good," she said. She didn't like it at all. Who would?

We were in church.
Everyone I knew was there,
elephants and pandas too.

The church was a cave.

A grave was there
and if you touched it
it would catch on fire.

There were tracks through the cave,
but if you touched the grave
the tracks would catch on fire.

A pit was there and you could fall in.
It wasn't deep, but you couldn't get out.

There were earthquakes and a grave,

a grave that made everything burn.

I dreamed it all night long.

In the end, we got out.
There was a slide
and we slid out. All of us—

except the burning grave.

~

Isn't church a place of safety and solace? Not anymore. This church is cold, creepy, underground—with a burning grave at its center. Everyone there is in danger.

Was the grave a hole in the ground? A mound with a tombstone? Was the coffin in it? I didn't ask, but one thing is clear: you must not touch this grave. It will torch you. It destroys everything, even the train tracks that should help you get around.

The cave has a pit; fall in, and you're trapped forever. Earthquakes roil the ground at your feet. Danger, all night long, DANGER! Yet . . . in a dramatic, miraculous rescue, we escape. All but one.

Dangers and dilemmas, reversals and contradictions. This child intuitively knows how much was lost. In time, she may say more. For now, I say: she caught the last slide out of childhood.

We all need a story to tell, as my daughter's dream makes clear. But the story is not given; we must construct it. We must make a story to tell ourselves and others what we lost, how we lost it, and what it all means. We must tell it, again and again, to make it real.

In traditional terms, this work is called mourning. Whatever its name, it is holy. All of it. The searing loss we feel when a loved one is ripped away. The shrine of words we make to tell the story of our loss. The caring listening of people who receive the story.

Making and telling the story of loss connects us to our deepest, most private experience; to other human beings; and the immense and silent mystery of God.

~

There came a day when I wrote these words:

> No understanding. No control. No Bill. These facts are now at the center of my life. If I am going to avoid losing my mind, I will have to use more than my mind to make sense of them.

This was North talking, orienting me—North, the soul's magnetic pole. I say this now, though it gets me ahead of myself, in order to say I was behind myself in understanding. I was trying to tell a story—to do the hard work of making meaning—with my wrecked self, my absent identity, the crushed person I became the day my brother died. To tell a meaningful story, I needed to build a new self.

Breathe, North seemed to be saying, as though it knew I was holding my breath. *Truth evolves. Your story will be told in different ways, in the many and varied ways you will frame it over time.*

WEST

Memory

3

THE OPEN DOOR

That sacred Closet when you sweep –
Entitled "Memory" –
Select a reverential Broom –
And do it silently –

Emily Dickinson

GRIEF

Grief is a room, invisible.
You are pushed into it.
For a while, it is the only
room in your house.

You stumble around.
No lights. No clocks.
No windows.
Empty.

When darkness is dark enough—
enough!—you cross
the threshold, return
to the visible world.

Dust on your desk,
on the fruit bowl.
Kitchen. Remember to eat.
Living room. Agree to talk.

When dust chafes
your living skin,
you'll step outside.
Sun and wind will be at play,

and you'll find yourself smiling.
Really, I mean find yourself—
you've been lost all this time.

You have the whole place back now,
but that room will always be there,
and the door will always be open.

The door to grief is always open.

When the wound is fresh, you're smacked off kilter. The very idea of absence confuses the brain.

Where sense leaves off, imagination fills in. You think you see your loved one at a window, in a doorway, in a crowd.

Objects and places dredge up memories and flash them.

Anniversaries come round with maddening regularity, returning you to the birthday, the death day, to holidays when every place at the table was filled.

As if this, all this, were not enough, you learn one more thing. Each death is connected to every other.

How could it be otherwise?

Grief's open door leads to memories.

We sweep there often.

Decked again.

Today it was the pan.

Home visiting my mother, six months after my brother's death, I reached into the pot closet for something to boil water in and pulled out an ancient pan. I was shocked to see my brother's signature on its side.

Then I remembered.

One day when Bill was about 10 years old, he found one of those electric pens that etches on glass and metal. I was in the kitchen on the morning he wrote his name—Billy McKernon—in wobbly letters as the pen skittered over the rounded metal surface.

Alone now in the same kitchen, I burst into tears—for Bill's name on the pan, his signature on bank loans, for all the ways he signed himself into and out of this life.

Our basement used to have music in it.

At our big sister's Sweet 16 party, she and her friends played 45s, got all shook up with Elvis, and sang bye-bye to love with the Everly Brothers. The year Bill was born, we twisted with Chubby Checker and built a stairway to heaven with Neil Sedaka. As the years spun by, we ran away with Del Shannon, went to the chapel with the Dixie Cups, cried there with Elvis, and held hands and hollered for help with the Beatles.

Eventually, the music moved upstairs to a stereo cabinet, a cassette boom box, and finally a CD player. By then, the basement held a tool bench, a washer and dryer, a pantry closet, a sewing machine, a water heater, and . . . one day . . . our brother, dying in silence.

LEAVING THE DRIVEWAY

Leaving the driveway,
   I furtively scanned
the basement window.

   I thought I saw you.
I know I felt you—as a boy
   waving sadly in the pane.

I wished the basement
   still had music in it.
The songs would

   wrap you like a blanket,
rock you like a mama,
   lift you and let you laugh—

be your arms, legs
  pulse and breath,
waft you up and out.

This next memory is blurry because I was 95 percent asleep when it happened, but the evidence remained all our lives. It was early morning, and I was in my teenage bed. My mother had tried several times to wake me for school, but I wanted to doze. Finally, she sent Bill in to get me up. By this time I was riled, and I swung my hand at him. When I finally did get up, I saw that I had scratched his cheek. Not intentionally, but I had scratched it. When his cut healed, it left a scar that he would wear for the rest of his life and that I would be ashamed of for the rest of mine.

It was the wiggly, fringy skirt that got him giggling. I don't remember exactly how old we were. Not kids anymore. Twenties, maybe? That's what made the game hilarious.

We were sitting at the kitchen table one evening when I was home for a visit. Just for fun, one of us made a hand lumber across the table like a brontosaurus, curving the four outer fingers down and lifting the middle finger slightly to make a long neck. This we had learned in childhood. We made other animals—a turtle, a fish, anything. We went on to people—a sleepy person, a hiccuping person, whoever came to mind. All of these we accompanied with sound effects. Then, his flash of inspiration: Bill became a skater, looping around, forward and backward, crisscrossing, making daring leaps, all the while humming "The Skaters' Waltz." I ran to find a notepad, scissors, and tape. Quickly I cut out a fringed skirt, taped it to my hand, and we waltzed our singing skaters around the oval rink.

Four months after Bill died, we had a wedding in the family. How strange to dress up and celebrate, not mourn. Mixed in with the festivities were memories of Bill's funeral and a powerful desire to have him with us.

PORTAL

Frank Capra's Version

I saw you enter the doorway
the bride and groom had crossed.

You appeared in your usual suit.
Your smile, your stride, were natural.

You scanned the room, found the table
with your wife, your children.

Like any other guest slipping in
amid clinking glasses and laughter,

you took your seat, the one
we've been saving for you.

What Really Happened

I saw you standing in the doorway
the bride and groom had crossed.

You appeared in your usual suit.
Shadows hid your face.

You scanned the room, saw the table
with your wife, your children.

But you stayed at the door,
and when I looked again later

you were gone.

One day, near the fourth anniversary of Bill's death, I was driving my younger daughter to her German lessons. We were talking about the Grimm stories when I noticed a hawk circling overhead.

At the sight of the hawk, I remembered the story of the six enchanted brothers turned to swans. Their sister saves them by knitting mantles out of nettles (German: *mantel,* coat). She suffers six years of silence and bleeding fingers. In the climactic scene, she is led to a stake, about to be burned to death. Her beloved swans come flying in. She flings a coat over each one's shoulders. This returns them to full human form—except the sixth brother, whose mantle is not quite finished. He is left with a swan's wing.

My stomach heaved. The swan-brother: He is himself, he is not. He is here, here is not. He is Bill. As they did four years ago, tears came now—flying down the highway, wanting to be the girl who saves her brother.

There was another brother I could not save. My memory of him reaches back to the defining event of my childhood. Perhaps if my family had been able to discuss what happened, I might not have gone off the rails when Bill died.

~

I am six years old, looking for Daddy.

"Maybe he's in our bedroom," Mommy says, "but be quiet, the baby's sleeping."

I go in, but Daddy isn't there. Mommy follows me into the room to look in on my new brother, Michael, almost three months old. "I'll just check on the little angel," she says. She picks him up.

"*Quick*," she says, "*find Daddy*." Her voice is scared and scary. She sends me next door, where I find him talking to our neighbor, and we run back home. Frightened voices. A phone call for an ambulance.

"Look at how blue," Mommy wails, "Oh, look at how blue!"

BLUE

The rescue team rushes in
the front door

and runs to the room where
my baby brother is.

One of the men carries
a metal tank. The handle

makes a clanking sound,
and they run so hard
the floor shakes.

Near me on the floor is
the only other person in

the living room: my other
little brother.

The pink one.

He is two years old,
sitting with his legs open,

stacking block on block
on block.

But I am the one

I am the one
in this room

who knows
that someone

in this house is
blue.

~

Many years later, while writing this book, I learned that the cause of Michael's death was streptococcal infection of the lungs. The pathologist's letter explained that strep can be fatal for an infant. But the letter arrived four months after Michael's death. With no obvious explanation in the meantime, the family doctor probably told my parents that Michael died of "crib death" (now called SIDS). Why the crib-death story persisted after the official letter arrived remains one of the family mysteries.

Also among the mysteries: how we felt. We just didn't talk about it. My father rarely mentioned it, except to say that perhaps a soul had needed a home for a few months. That idea didn't work for my mother. She clung to Michael, to his life and death. She set his photograph on her dresser, where it stayed for the next 50 years, and she talked about him whenever people asked about her children.

Every time she told the story, I was returned to the night Michael died. When he disappeared, that is. I mean, he vanished. Here one minute, gone the next. I could not make sense of it. In what world can it be natural for a baby to just . . . die? Not for me, in this one. Not in the next, either. No story made sense. Not crib death. Not pneumonia. Not "it was his time to be with God," which they likely told us.

Not that I could reason abstractly about death at age six. What was real for me? The shock. The gut-level wound. The darkness that night. Fear of a ghost. Our sadness. My aloneness. Michael's absence. The suddenness of his absence. The unendingness of his absence. The truest words: "Well, kids, you just lost your little brother."

My missing baby brother has been with me all my life. How could he not be? On the night Michael died, I became aware of myself as a separate person. This dreadful knowledge—the loneliness of privacy—marked the end of my childhood. And the shocking experience of sudden death marked the beginning of my one true obsession—present absence, absent presence—the paradox at the heart of grief.

In this line of dots

. . . .

where does the eye want to look?

We can hold loved ones like beads on the heart's string. But how can we hold their absence? How can we believe it?

Here's Dickinson, in a letter, just after her father died: "that Pause of Space which I call 'Father'." Again, two years later: "I dream about father every night, always a different dream, and forget what I am doing daytimes, wondering where he is. Without any body, I keep thinking. What kind can that be?"

We have to think the word *body* in order to think *no body*.

What is nothing, in itself?

zero
lack   void
without   nowhere
disappeared   vacant
anonymous   separation
hollow   craving
not   can't
-less   un-
empty   unknown
hole   invisible
never   hiatus
mute   surrender
vacuum   lost
extinct   blank
gone

Does any of this make sense?

How to understand the absence of someone? The disappearance of your former self? The lack of normal? The *nothingness* of nothing?

I once saw a candle in a cut-glass holder, a beautiful little flower-shaped cup with beveled petals that cast out bars of darkness and wedges of light. In the flickering silence, I felt it: loss is a dark star, a pattern of absence, an invisible radiance. The missing person is the only one who fits between the wedges of light, who has that missing shape, who reaches out with absent arms.

A memory is a placeholder. It has the size and weight and shape of a missing person. For a moment, you can feel it in your hand. For the long moment of memory.

NORTH

Healing

4

TURNING TOWARD NORTH

Bulletins from Immortality

Emily Dickinson

My brother was now a memory. How was I to heal when the loss was so sudden, so inexplicable? Without him I felt shocked, disoriented, aimless, alone, angry, lost. In a word, crazy.

Crazy ricochets from foolish (it was a crazy thing to do) to ardent (he's crazy about her) to temporarily out of control (he went crazy on me) to kooky (she has some crazy ways) to insane (he needs a shrink—he's crazy). As it turns out, the root of the word *crazed* means crushed, cracked, broken.

To my crushed, cracked, broken self, my brother's suicide was huge. Like an object held too close to the eyes, it clogged my mental field and overshadowed everything else. Yet, over time, the loss seemed to shrink. As Dickinson put it, "the Tomb / Like other new Things – shows largest – then – / And smaller, by Habit –."

But which loss was I gaining perspective on? There were two.

One was the loss of my brother. To distance myself, I had to make it real—on all levels. I had to convince myself that he died (no, he's not that man over there). I had to tell, again and again, the facts (this is how he died; that is how we went on). I had to hone a pithy explanation for acquaintances (it was a medication meltdown). I had to construct an understanding of how this could have happened (   ). This last blank is taking a long time to fill in.

The other loss was the person I was on the day before my brother died. As Dickinson put it: "Something's odd – within – / That person that I was – / And this One – do not feel the same – / Could it be Madness – this?" To gain distance from that person—and avoid losing my mind—I had to let my old self recede into the past. I had to make a new, healing self that would stumble into the future.

Is a person one thing, single? Or do parts of the self, like tendrils, latch on to truths until finally the whole self heaves into a new center?

And if so, how?

It was the next day, the morning after the news of Bill's suicide. I was looking out the kitchen window, feeling angry at him for leaving so suddenly, willfully, singly—he, just himself. What was he thinking? Of his children, all five of them? His wife? His mother? His brothers, sisters? How could he!

Anger, flaming anger.

Then.

I heard a voice.

"Try to understand," it said. The sound was distinctly Bill's, speaking calmly but firmly. "*Try to understand.*"

It stopped me, cooled me, steadied me. It was like the thought that came to me days later at the funeral—*You are not the star*—but there was a difference. That was a thought, but this was the sound of Bill's voice. The voice was not coming from outside me, but its timbre and resonance were authentic, true to the sound I knew and loved.

This was my first experience, after Bill's death, of the place on the compass I call North. I won't dwell on the question of what the voice was or where it came from. The eminent neurologist Oliver Sacks would have called this an auditory hallucination, and so do I. Yet I also call it grace. It rescued me. It set me on a path through the wilderness, the path that led to this writing. The main event, for me, is the mystery of how I moved forward after devastation. How anyone does.

My progress came in a series of turning points, as if I were rounding a corner. Turning was not simple or easy, not necessarily conscious or even comprehensible. It was a switchback trail up from the bottom of a crater.

My turning points often surprised me. They were like the Magic 8 Ball. When I was a girl I had this toy, which pretends to answer questions put to it. The ball is black, about four inches in diameter, with a numeral 8 on top. It resembles the eight-ball in billiards, though I didn't know this at the time. I cared about the words that appeared in a window at the bottom of the ball. The words were inscribed on a floating triangle that bobbled around in liquid and rose to the surface to reveal answers suggesting yes, no, or uncertainty. I had no end of fun with this toy, though I knew it could only produce words already written.

I think of the Magic 8 Ball in connection with North because thoughts came to me in a similar way. Like Dickinson's bulletins from immortality, they floated up and presented answers fitted precisely to the questions; in some cases, they presented questions that challenged me. These thoughts could come at any time and in any medium—words, images, dreams, truths I didn't know I knew, even a physical experience that triggered an understanding.

Two months after my brother's death, this question came to me:

Can not having a house <u>be</u> a house?

I had been turning, tumbling over in my mind Emily Dickinson's ecstatic poem that begins "I dwell in Possibility – / A fairer House than Prose." In the sky-high house of possibility, she said, she spreads wide her narrow hands to gather paradise.

I had no house. I had instead a jelly-like state.

I grew up in Connecticut on Long Island Sound. I had often seen jellyfish stranded on the sand at low tide. Even a jellyfish has a shape, but I felt no shape at all. No outer edge, no container, no definition.

Customary thoughts—replaced.

Customary beliefs—evaporated.

Customary family—ruptured.

Customary comforts—gone.

Customary strategies—not working.

Customary work—impossible.

Yet this thought—*Can not having a house be a house?*—had perspective. It was a way of saying, "Right now, I have no shape. That's the shape I'm in."

One morning, I went to one of the most consoling places I knew: the Basilica of St. Mary in Minneapolis. This was the day before the three-month anniversary of Bill's death. I say this because, in the beginning, I needed to keep track of time by that date, February 4. In its way, this was like charting a baby's growth: first in weeks, then in months, later in years.

I took my baby self to the basilica to cry. In my raw, disoriented state, this lasted some time. When the tears subsided, I took paper and pencil and wrote whatever words came to mind. They dribbled out slowly, drops from a weepy faucet, and they didn't make sense. They seemed weird to me, as my daughter's dream had seemed to her. I wrote them anyway, just as they came, in this order:

breathe

tears

lonesome

in

here

accept

wound

open

is

good

When I got home, I took out the page and looked again. This time I saw something like a telegram. No, wait—two telegrams.

Prayer: "Breathe tears. Lonesome in here."

Response: "Accept wound. Open is good."

IN THE BASILICA

I went to the basilica because it had steps to climb
  before I entered it.

I went to the basilica because no one I knew was there.
  I did not want casual conversation.

I went to the basilica because it was vast.
  Its ceiling was high, its walls distant.
    I could feel my smallness.

I went to the basilica because it echoed. My tiniest sighs
  carried. They breathed into the distance and returned
    magnified, accepted.

I went to the basilica because it was a womb. In it,
  I could feel my own emptiness and curl into the silence.

I went to the basilica because its silence was open, living.
  If I sat within it long enough, an interior quiet settled in,
    enfolded by the outer, and it was full.

I went to the basilica because I would know when
  I was ready to leave.

I went to the basilica because it had steps to step down
  before I reentered the world.

Four months after my brother's death, I was on an escalator in a department store. It was a double staircase, the up and down stairs set side by side under a skylight. Like all escalators, it was tricky. Steps appear out of one floor and disappear into the next. Split-second timing is required. A smooth transition or a fall, those are the options. It's all in the balance of trust and caution.

I was mulling over the questions. How could he die so alone, bereft of friends and family, of prayer and aid and solace? There, on the escalator, riding with other people—some going up, some down, all side by side in the light—these words came to me: *sovereign will.*

I saw—going up, going down, in the light—this was Bill's choice, to end his pain. Going up, going down, he threw himself off. Going up, going down, in the light all around. He got off.

His choice.

This was not a new answer. It was ancient—free will—but the word *sovereign* was mine. Sovereign will, the prerogative of God and kings, is ours as well.

This was not a comforting answer, but it fit the most vexing hole in the puzzle: *If the will to live is primal, how did he choose death? Did he, in fact, choose it?* The fact was obvious, but I had denied it—so earnestly that a trusted friend had had to say to me, gently, "Most people who kill themselves mean to do it."

So. I knew bad things happen to good people, but I had to experience that truth to know it. I knew we make our own choices, but I had to feel that truth to get it. The answer on the escalator did not dissolve the paradox—my brother's death chose him as fiercely as he chose it—but it allowed me to see both sides simultaneously.

"The Soul should always stand ajar," Dickinson said. Nowhere is the soul more open than in dreams. I had an especially vivid series of dreams starting about a year and a half after Bill's death. They seemed to reveal growth that I was unable to sense or accept in any other way. Often the main characters took nonhuman form.

i

I am visiting my childhood home, now covered in cobwebs. Spiders have taken over the crumbling house. I rig up a cottony pom-pom to break their webs and take back each room, but the spiders are determined to battle me. It is personal between us. Are they protecting something? One of the spiders turns toward me, glares fiercely, and seems to want to speak.

WEBBING

The house
  of your childhood
    is crumbling,
my work,
  urgent

  I zig-
zag, criss-
  cross each room,
    inch over
the territory
with all my legs
    risk
  falling

I spin
these lines
out of my own body
tie them
to the walls
of your first home
connect them catch
memories

You don't know
how to love me
yet I know
how to save you
Many times
you have wanted
to kill me
but I
will not
let you

Fierce tender
warrior I am
you

ii

In an old house, I discover a small room covered with wood paneling. I want to remove the paneling for a more natural feel. I pull off a section and find insects in the wall, devouring the house. Horrified, I try to fit the paneling back on, but the insects crawl swiftly over my arms and body. They want me—even my skin, my most intimate boundary. I think mindless, mindless!

DECONSTRUCTION CREW

All legs and pincers
mouth and motion,

we are chewing on the
premises of your mind.

Core concepts,
foundation principles—

you want them but
you don't need them.

We'll digest them all,
make room in here

for doubt to edify
your soul.

iii

Two years after my brother's death, I was asked to give a talk about poems I'd found helpful in my experience with grief. And the title? "A Wiser Sympathy," I said, taking a phrase from one of Dickinson's grief poems. This, I had planned. Then, spontaneously, a subtitle occurred to me: "Points on the Compass of Grief." No hesitation. The concept appeared fully formed, as if it had been waiting for me to express it, though I hadn't a clue the moment before. As if I had been living it already.

Planning the talk stirred up strong emotions. One week before the presentation, I had a powerful dream that crystallized the meaning of North. It still feels, after all these years, like a gift.

A young woman has lost one of her fingers in an accident, but she does not want to reattach it. She considers the loss a necessary sacrifice and feels she must go on suffering. Bill is there and urges her to get the finger reattached. She keeps resisting, he keeps insisting.

A small poem emerged from this dream, a dialogue between the severed finger and the woman's hand. *Please,* the finger says, *let yourself be stitched back together.*

SCARRING

Dip me in salt!
Put me on ice!
Take me to the doctor!

When we're attached
how will I know
you were ever missing?

Stitches will mend.
You'll have a ring.
A scar will be our token.

iv

Again, I am in my parents' house. As I settle down to sleep,

I discover that the ceiling is not a ceiling; the house is entirely open to a brilliant night sky. The stars have fanciful shapes, and they're active, alive. I know I am seeing this for the first time.

LUCID DARKNESS

I lie down to sleep
on the living room floor
of my childhood home.

I look up to find
no roof but the sky alight,
stars deep in play.

Pinwheels!
Helixes!
Asterisks!

This is how heaven
appears to a mind
made lucid by darkness.

5

FAITH, DOUBT, AND THE NAKED FOOT

On subjects of which we know nothing . . .
we both believe, and disbelieve
a hundred times an Hour,
which keeps Believing nimble.

Emily Dickinson

IN THE DARKNESS

This
prayer
would
tap
like a
red-
tipped
cane

I bow
before the
mystery
of boundless
grace and
compassion

I gave
over my
precious
mind
to this
slender
rod
and got
each day
a plot
where I
could
place a

single
naked
foot

The God part. Belief. Unbelief. Doubt. Faith.

These things were deep in my life before, during, and after my brother's death. So, like everything else, they had to be known in a new way. Dickinson was the perfect companion for me in this work. God, to her, was everything from a father to a swindler, an illegible force to an eclipse, an avalanche to an avenue, a marauding hand to an abiding friend. She didn't settle for one image, one answer.

What was the ground I stood on? Humility was my acre to till. I did not know this at first. At first, I stood on the field and snarled at God. Why had things not happened differently? Why are some sufferers rescued, some not? It was a big field, dark and still.

Before me was a challenge: to give up wanting to know. Beyond that challenge was another: to give up assuming that I could know. Here, there were cues from Dickinson. On a light note, she said she avoided people because of the thoughtless way they toss around sacred terms and topics: "they talk of Hallowed things, aloud – and embarrass my Dog –." On a deeper level, in a crisis, she wrote a letter-poem for her sister-in-law, Sue. Sue's eight-year-old son, Gib—the darling of the family—had died suddenly of typhoid fever, and Sue's devout religious convictions were put to the test. In response, Dickinson wrote "Faith is *Doubt.*"

These paradoxical words are worth puzzling over. I can begin by saying that, for me, faith and doubt have always coexisted. But are they opposites? Are they locked in a zero-sum game, each one's gain the other's loss? Dickinson seemed to be saying no.

I'd rather call doubt by another name: disbelief. I had to disbelieve some notions and ditch some terms and topics. This work has been going on all my life. There is, and always has been, a deconstruction crew at work in my soul. But disbelieving became urgent in this crisis. To recover from my brother's suicide, I had to give up believing in belief.

The jingle of its anklet.

Constructing an image of an elephant

from the chime of its distant bells.

The satisfactions of the blind mind.

That is how preposterous religious belief seemed to me.

Yet as time went on, I had to give up disbelief—erasing the elephant—and, with it, the congratulations of the rational mind. I had to rely on faith, the high-wire act where the soul becomes a foot.

PRAYER OF THE FOOT

Don't give me eyes.
Don't give me ears.
Only let me feel a path
as I lay my sole upon it.
Let me praise my maker
for toes, heels
cathedral arches
and the grace to bear
a battered body
across a narrow beam.

Doubt and faith belong together. They are the falling out-of and into relation. So intertwined, they are one. This is my understanding of Dickinson's line, "Faith is *Doubt*."

If I had to say what doubt is, in and of itself, I'd say it's the unbalance that balances faith.

If I had to say what faith is, in and of itself, I'd say it's the foot on the beam, the precarious journey, the traveling-with.

This way of walking was not given in a blinding flash. It grew slowly, quietly, like meadow grass. I began to bow, to acknowledge: I am small, embedded in a vast maker-web in which my tiny *I* is a mere cross-hatch. There are answers my little knot cannot be given and was never designed to know.

I began to embrace Silence, to make of myself a cup to hold mystery.

Cup cup cupping my tea this morning. The comfort is in the holding. Just want to hold the cup and feel its warmth along the curve of my palm. A small gesture that feels complete and . . . mine. After ten days of travel and visiting, I need to reset, return to myself. And so I sit quietly in my corner. Hold my cup, write a few words. Hold, write.

This morning, I need a simple presence, a single breath. Rumi: "Feel this breathing." It was good, while away, to read Rumi. Leave Dickinson at home, where she would prefer to be, and open to another voice that tells me the soul is a mirror. If it has a shape, it is a cup.

A vessel of mysteries. Who or what reminded me *You are not the star* as I cowered in my pew at my brother's funeral? Who or what tossed up the words *sovereign will* when I was on the escalator? Who or what remembered the words of the minister who said that my brother's keepers were weeping beside him? I could not accept his words at the time; why did I tuck them away, as a squirrel treasures his nut? Some part of me was listening, like a child behind a door swung slightly ajar. Whoever and whatever it is, this quietly breathing self was always present.

Being—this multiple be-ing—goes on in layers, out of range of the conscious mind, like districts of a city. Some parts are ancient. Some are newly built. Some are refurbished in period style with modern conveniences. Part of me may be running the city council while another is managing the garbage dump—or, sometimes, being the dump.

I don't always know who's in charge at the moment. Yet the whole has a wisdom that the parts do not have. Who or what hears and knows when something that matters is being said? How does the soul know when it's being nourished? I can't say. But I know this: from time to time, someone whispers a message. Or somebody spots wisdom, rings the bell on the church steeple and shouts, "Heads up! Truth is here."

Somehow, the whole self knows how to gather the flung and flailing parts, make new parts, and create another identity. The new person, like any other created thing, seems to come out of nowhere—like the wheel. After the wheel was invented, it seemed simple and obvious. Before it was invented, it was not: not simple, not obvious, not there. Just so after loss. The old self has gone missing, but the new self isn't present; it has not yet been created. The new self needs to learn:

Normal is what you have because you live it.

6

ACCEPT WOUND, OPEN IS GOOD

Do not try to be saved –
but let Redemption find you –
as it certainly will –

Emily Dickinson

I had to live my way into a new normal—accept my wounded state and move forward while bereaved. It's worth taking a moment to think about the word *bereaved* to understand just how complicated healing is.

Bereaved has deep historical roots. Its grandfathers are the Old English words *reafian* (to plunder) and *bereafian* (to take away). Related words include *rob*, *rout*, *usurp* and a gangster family of *-rupts*: *abrupt*, *bankrupt*, *corrupt*, *disrupt*, *erupt*, *interrupt*, and *rupture*. In fact, the mother of this tree of battle-axes is the Indo-European root that means to snatch. Does the word *rip-off* come to mind?

In the crisis of grief, I wanted to shout, "Stop, thief! Avenge the rip-off! Save the victim!" But is grief something to be corrected, solved, or disappeared? It's time to say what grief is. But better first to say what grief is not. In my experience, grief is not sadness, anger, loneliness, confusion, fear, or depression. It can involve these things, some or all of them, but it is not these things. It concerns loss, but it is not loss. Grief is itself. It is not reducible to anything else.

Grief is the suffering we experience after great loss. We give it this name because no other word will do. With its Latin root, *gravis*, it speaks of the grave and the solemn burden of loss. Grief is at the heart of being human because it involves the human heart. The heart's deep love. Its unbearable loss. Its shattering. Its resilience. Its utter privacy. Its hunger for community. Its ordinariness. Its holiness.

Grief is the search for a lost loved one.

Grief is the search for a lost self.

Grief is a wilderness trekked by a barefoot heart.

Grief is a holy madness.

~

Holy. Sacred. These powerful words evoke images of God, religion, spirituality, ritual, meditation, and prayer. They also illuminate grief. Though they're used interchangeably, they come from different languages and offer two windows—one on healing, the other on loss.

The word *holy* provides a window on healing. *Holy* comes from Old English (*halig*), and its root means whole. Wholeness conveys the sense of health (think *hale*) and freedom from injury or recovery from it; in a word, wellbeing. After a loss, your entire self—extended to the outermost, invisible horizon—is seeking wellbeing through healing.

Healing resembles phototropism, the arc of leaf toward light. It's a turning toward life, a reorienting. This is the work I call North.

You are alive, North says. *You have life's power in you. You heal the way your body heals, organically. With your body, you are always growing and repairing. Healing must be lived—lived with, lived into, lived for. Life itself will heal you.*

I am larger than life, North says. *I am your soul's magnetic pole, and I am larger than your soul. I knit you together in your mother's womb. I have your wholeness at heart. I am Wholeness itself, evolving. I am with you when you cannot see me, feel me, taste me. I speak when you least expect me. And I tell you: Accept wound. Open is good.*

~

After my brother's death, I lost my sense of wholeness. I lost sleep. I lost energy. I lost concentration. I lost my appetite. I lost my sense of time. I lost my sense of humor. I lost patience for daily pleasantries. I lost listening to music; it seemed contrived. I lost count of how many things I lost. So many parts of me were missing, I lost my balance.

Balance, wholeness. Each is essential to the other. When you think of a body in motion—a dancer or an athlete, say—arms are moving, legs are moving, the entire body is moving, perhaps twisting, spinning. There's a center of gravity that balances all parts in all planes. The center is the one point that gathers all the others. It must be rediscovered every moment because the body moves. If this sounds complicated, it is. Yet babies do it every day; that's why they're called toddlers. They're struggling to shift their sense of balance from sitting to standing, then from standing to moving forward while upright. Every day, they get up and do it all over again until they get the hang of it.

The same is true after loss. Normal goes missing and your life changes shape. Everything is out of relation and you need a new balance point. This is sacred work. Sacred—there's that halo again, this time around the people and things we love. Treasured objects, like children's blankies and stuffed animals, fit in this category because they're loved like no other. The word *sacred*, in its Latin root, means set apart, declared special. This gives us a window on loss.

Sacred is the place where your heart is fixed. Your world revolves around it. Here you find balance and ease; here you are refreshed and restored. In this private place of joy and solace, you are centered. In this place of balance, you sense God: the Holy Oneness that holds all of you. Your broken places. Your missing parts. Your garbage dump. Your strength. Your beauty. Your uniqueness.

You loved a particular person, a sacred someone set apart from all others. Beautiful. Irreplaceable. When you lost that person, you lost the place where your heart was fixed. The uniqueness and beauty of the one you lost makes your grieving sacred. The uniqueness and privacy of your grieving makes your healing sacred. Each life is sacred, including your own.

Grief is sacred. Grief is holy. Grief can also be perilous.

Dickinson wrote about "dangerous moments" that occur "when the meaning goes out of things . . . If we survive them they expand us . . ." To survive the dangerous moment of my brother's suicide, I needed to stretch—in two directions.

I needed to expand my idea of loss. To feel around inside it and ask whether emptiness can be positive. To see whether I could believe Dickinson when she said "'Nothing' is the force / That renovates the World –."

I also needed to reach out to others. To risk connecting with people who had lost someone. To receive and give what Dickinson called a wiser sympathy.

These two, I found, are related.

THE SOMETHING OF NOTHING

cup lap
room alcove
chalice hearth
vase tub
womb

quiet solitude
vacation weekend
creativity insight
pause sabbath
rest

welcome courtesy
discretion invitation
listening admiration
helping introducing
tact apology
respect

hope love
humility faith
generosity sacrifice
kindness patience
forgiveness forbearance
compassion

All of these no-things are powerful and positive. Anything with an open boundary—small or large, kettle or stadium—opens to receive. Respite from routine restores us and opens us to new possibilities. The social graces make room for other people and keep us connected. Spiritual virtues ennoble our lives and make us deeper vessels.

Yet the greatest of all, in my experience of healing, is listening. Like the basilica, with its living silence, listening creates a space for someone to curl into and be held. Listening is the most delicate form of reaching out. It is the simplest and most powerful thing we can do for one another.

FOUR PEOPLE WHO LISTENED

i

Soon after my brother's funeral, I went to my doctor for an annual physical. The medical information form needed updating, and one of the first questions was about siblings—how many? There was my loss in black and white. I began to sob. My doctor reached across the desk and took my hand. "Talk to me," she said, and listened compassionately as my words and tears poured out.

ii

Months later, I had a heart-to-heart with a good friend. I asked—I was still asking—why my brother died. She listened all through dinner. Then, slowly and quietly, she said, "Your brother's death will always be a deep, deep mystery." So. She blessed it, all of it: his awful death, my anguish, my family's turmoil, the whole catastrophe. She gave it the dignity it deserved.

iii

Another good friend wept, actually wept, when I showed her

my brother's picture. His face was open, intelligent, kind. "See," I said, "see what we lost."

iv

From time to time, one of the ministers from my church would call to ask how I was doing. Mostly, she listened. One day she said, "There is something powerful in you, working for your redemption." I was so startled, I wrote down her words. Except for *redemption*, she hadn't used lofty religious language. The words I responded to were *something powerful in you, working*. Construction was going on, and heavy lifting.

~

I treasure these saving moments. I call them saving *moments* because there was not one big save. There were small moments of large blessing, bestowed when people truly listened and simply held my grief. They held me where I was, as I was.

I think again of my daughter's dream, when we escaped the burning church-cave. There was a slide and we slid out. We left the cave, all of us, together. How do we leave the cave? We leave together by listening. We hold each other's stories and help one another move forward. This is a collective form of North. The receiving doesn't need to be fancy or wise. Simplicity, I learned, does well: a gesture (a hand clasp or caring expression) or a few words ("I'm thinking of you"). In fact, the less said or done, the better. This is Dickinson's wiser sympathy, a quiet respect for grief. Just let it be, not question it. Receive it, not try to fix it.

WHEN YOU MEET SOMEONE DEEP IN GRIEF

Slip off your needs
and set them by the door.

Enter barefoot
this darkened chapel

hollowed by loss
hallowed by sorrow

its gray stone walls
and floor.

You, congregation
of one

are here to listen
not to sing.

Kneel in the back pew.
Make no sound,

let the candles
speak.

Afterword

BLESSING GRIEF

I will not let thee go except I bless thee

Emily Dickinson

All night they wrestled, the biblical patriarch Jacob and a mysterious, divine man. When dawn came and they were still at it, Jacob declared, "I will not let thee go, except thou bless me."

Dickinson reversed his words. Shortly before her death, she wrote to her literary friend Thomas Higginson, "Audacity of Bliss, said Jacob to the Angel 'I will not let thee go except I bless thee' – Pugilist and Poet, Jacob was correct –." Looking back, she pronounced a farewell blessing on their friendship and her writing.

This is what I do for grief.

I've wrestled with it. Written thousands of words about it. Walked around, across, upon it. In the end, I bless it. I say it is beautiful. It is more than beautiful. It is holy.

In the end, though there is no end, I bless my friendship with my brother. I say I am grateful for all he gave me and all that he was. His death is part—only a part—of his wholeness.

THE GREAT BENEVOLENCE

Your tree
in close-up is a weeping willow
in long shot, a flaming maple
far in the distance, one among many
in a forest of suicides
Dante told us there was no redemption—
the spirit twists forever in
the woody form of failure
But I say peace, peace—
in the great benevolence
everything is reclaimed
For you, there will be soft earth at the root
summer and winter birds
blue and gray sky above
and the gradual blessing of all that lives
branch by twig
cell by atom
return

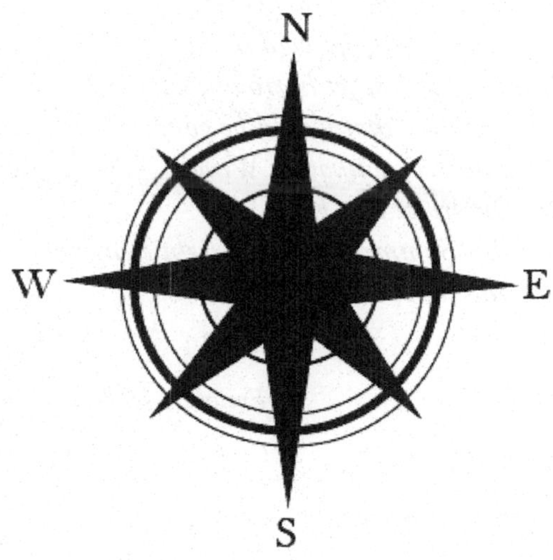
N
W
E
S

As imperceptibly as Grief
The Summer lapsed away –
Too imperceptible at last
To seem like Perfidy –
A Quietness distilled
As Twilight long begun,
Or Nature spending with herself
Sequestered Afternoon –
The Dusk drew earlier in –
The Morning foreign shone –
A courteous, yet harrowing Grace,
As Guest, that would be gone –
And thus, without a Wing
Or service of a Keel
Our Summer made her light escape
Into the Beautiful –

Emily Dickinson

Dickinson begins this poem on the slant, as if it were about summer, which it so slyly is. Subtly, she distracts us from grief by shifting our attention to summer's gradual death. Of course, she doesn't use the word *death*; that would be too obvious.

Summer simply lapses, as if we hadn't noticed. Dickinson could have said slipped, the root meaning of lapse. But *lapse* dovetails with *perfidy* and suggests faithlessness; it's also a word used when a contract ends through neglect. All of these meanings braided together imply disloyalty, the willful breach of a relationship. Could this be true?

Summer can't tell us. It's so far gone, it's imperceptible. In its place is a profound quietness, the essence of rest (*distilled*). It's the stillness we feel as day fades to darkness. Or is it how nature enjoys its own presence? Then again, *sequester* is a legal term used when disputed property is handed over to a third party; a nod to the way we wrangle with death.

Days are shorter now, and morning light slants strangely low and golden. Summer's departure is gracious, yet painful; this beloved guest will not overstay her welcome. The phrase *harrowing grace* is rich in associations. In Dickinson's time, the farming tool called a harrow used rows of spikes to pulverize the soil and prepare it for planting. By combining images of spikes and seeds, she leads us to the sharp pain of loss and the physical act of burial. Linking harrowing to grace, she suggests that the work has a higher purpose.

Not driven away, not destroyed, not abandoned—summer has left voluntarily, like a bird flown from the nest or a ship bound for sea. In fact, summer has escaped, slipped out of its cloak, the root meaning of the word. Like a cultivated plant species that begins to grow in the wild (another meaning of *escape*), summer slips out of hand and makes off for the Beautiful. What or where is the Beautiful? Dickinson doesn't say. She implies, though, that summer has gone to a place of pleasure and delight.

Summer has returned to what she always was. Her escape is light: graceful, unburdened, cheerful. She's traveling light and taking her light with her. Our grief at her loss also fades, just as naturally. She was Our Summer when she was with us and ours still when she's gone. No relationship has been breached. Our love abides, and grief has been transformed.

This book is my witness to abiding love and transformation. I've tracked loss and healing, a doe and her fawn. I've seen their hoof prints—in the snow, in the mud. I've found where they nest, where they drink. I've fed them patience. I've watched them in the dark and in the light.

"The Truth must dazzle gradually / Or every man be blind –," Dickinson wrote. Grief is just as dazzling. It is a madness that makes divinest sense. The truths it reveals cannot be known all at once; they must be seen on the slant of time.

One of the most powerful truths I learned was that the loftiest part of myself was always on duty. It was present despite the chaos, within the chaos. Present wherever I wandered, whatever I found: snake or squirrel, bee or bone, rock or razor.

In the place I call North, I felt found, rescued, met, known, led, righted, given to, bestowed upon, inspired—all words claimed by religious tradition. What do *you* call this place? What is its center? For me, North is the soul's magnetic pole; the divine is its compass, nothing less. For you, it may be the regenerative power of life; that, in itself, is majestic.

I leave you with a compass and a wilderness. They are not a theory. They are images that came from experience. They say, this is what my grief looked like, felt like. They say, this is how it was to wander through it. They ask, is this your grief, too?

"The 'hand you stretch me in the Dark,' I put mine in," Dickinson wrote.

Here is my hand, reaching for yours.

NOTES

Are you a digger, like me? If so, these notes will help you find the poems and letters referenced in *Grief's Compass*, read them for yourself, and discover your own meaning.

Quotations from Dickinson's poems are taken from R.W. Franklin's reading edition. Thomas H. Johnson's edition is not quoted, but his poem numbers are included for readers who have his collection.

Quotations from Dickinson's letters are taken from Thomas H. Johnson's one-volume edition. Dates are also given for readers who may have other sources for the letters.

Alternative words for poems are taken from Cristanne Miller's annotated edition of Dickinson's handbound and unbound poems.

In a few cases, I have followed Miller's practice of quietly changing Dickinson's spelling so as not to distract the reader.

~

The Poems of Emily Dickinson. Reading Edition. Ed. R.W. Franklin. Cambridge, Massachusetts: The Belknap Press of Harvard University Press, 1999.

The Complete Poems of Emily Dickinson. Ed. Thomas H. Johnson. Boston: Little, Brown and Company, 1960.

The Letters of Emily Dickinson. Single-volume edition. Ed. Thomas H. Johnson and Theodora Ward. Cambridge, Massachusetts: The Belknap Press of Harvard University Press, 1986.

Emily Dickinson's Poems: As She Preserved Them. Ed. Cristanne Miller. Cambridge, Massachusetts: The Belknap Press of Harvard University Press, 2016.

This is how the poems are referenced: First, after the page number, a brief form of the quotation in the text of *Grief's Compass.* Next, the poem's scholarly numbers, one for each of the two standard sources for the complete poems: Franklin-number / Johnson-number. Last, the first line of the poem. Knowing the first line can be especially helpful when searching because Dickinson did not title her poems; scholars refer to a poem by its first line and/or the number given to it.

Letters are referenced similarly. First, after the page number, a brief form of the quotation. Next, the scholarly number and the recipient. Last, the date.

~

FOREWORD

1. A Wilderness of Size. In poem F-1092 / J-856 (There is a finished feeling)
3. Oates, Joyce Carol. "The Deadly Sins/Despair; The One Unforgivable Sin." *New York Times*, July 25, 1993, Sunday Book Review.
3. There is a pain – so utter. Poem F-515 / J-599 (There is a pain so utter)

   Dickinson wrote alternatives for some of the words in her poems, apparently without choosing which ones she considered definitive (dwelling in possibility, as she so famously said). In this poem, Dickinson wrote *Being* as an alternate for *substance*, *steady* for *safely*, and *spill Him* for *drop Him.* If I had seen the phrase "swallows Being up" when I first read this poem, I would have grasped the meaning more easily, but then I wouldn't have dug for understanding. I note the variants so that you, as a reader, can mull the possibilities.

4. The Wilderness is new – to you. In letter 517 to T.W. Higginson (September 1877)
4. Her ragged, barefoot heart. In letter 966 to Mrs. J.G. Holland (February 1885)
5. Much Madness is divinest Sense. In poem F-620 / J-435 (Much madness is divinest sense). And so I say that grief is a holy madness.

CHAPTER 1

9. I, and Silence, some strange Race. In poem F-340 / J-280 (I felt a funeral in my brain)
12. Bewilderness. I found this perfect word in Frederick Buechner's *Telling Secrets*.
13. An Element of Blank. In poem F-760 / J-650 (Pain has an element of blank)
13. The pain so utter. In poem F-515 / J-599 (There is a pain so utter)
20. Grief is a Mouse. Poem F-753 / J-793 (Grief is a mouse)

    Dickinson also wrote the word *embers* as a possible substitute for *ashes*, and *an answer* for *a syllable*. I like *embers* very much because it conjures the image of grief flaring up again.

CHAPTER 2

25. And grateful that a thing / So terrible – had been endured. In poem F-423 / J-410 (The first day's night had come)
29. We grow accustomed to the Dark, and the following stanza. In poem F-428 / J-419 (We grow accustomed to the dark)
30. As if / His Mind were going blind, and the following lines. In poem F-994 / J-1062 (He scanned it – staggered)
30. Never Bud from a Stem. In poem F-975 / J-913 (And this of all my hopes)

    Dickinson may have been thinking of a Bible passage, Jonah 4:6-10. In this part of the story, God makes a vine grow and then creates a worm to destroy it, all to teach Jonah that

CHAPTER 6

89. Do not try to be saved. In letter 522 to T.W. Higginson (early autumn 1877)

91. Grief as a wilderness, in letter 517 to T.W. Higginson (September 1877). Barefoot heart, in letter 966 to Mrs. J.G. Holland (February 1885). Holy madness suggested by the line "Much Madness is divinest Sense," in poem F-620 / J-435; and "Could it be Madness – this?" from poem F-423 / J-410 (The first day's night had come)

92. I knit you together in your mother's womb. Psalm 139:13 (NIV): "For you created my inmost being; you knit me together in my mother's womb."

94. Dangerous moments. In prose fragment 49 (PF 49), *Letters*, p. 919

94. "Nothing" is the force / That renovates the World. In poem F-1611 / J-1563 (By homely gifts and hindered words)

94. A wiser sympathy. In poem F-780 / J-743 (The birds reported from the south)

AFTERWORD

101. I will not let thee go except I bless thee. In letter 1042 to T.W. Higginson (spring 1886)

103. Jacob wrestles with the divine man and asks for a blessing. Genesis 32:24-29 (KJV)

103. Audacity of Bliss, said Jacob to the Angel. In letter 1042 to T.W. Higginson (spring 1886)

103. Walked around, across, upon grief. Words from poem F-515 / J-599 (There is a pain so utter)

106. As imperceptibly as Grief. Poem F-935 / J-1540 (As imperceptibly as grief)

An early version of this poem included more stanzas, but the one presented here was Dickinson's retained copy and the version she sent to Thomas Higginson. This four-stanza version is also the one published by Johnson and Franklin. The other stanzas are included in Cristanne Miller's collection, where she notes one minor word substitution (*unto* for *into*) written in the early version of the final stanza.

109. The Truth must dazzle gradually. In poem F-1263 / J-1129 (Tell all the truth but tell it slant)

109. A madness that makes divinest sense. In poem F-620 / J-435 (Much madness is divinest sense)

109. The hand you stretch me in the Dark. In letter 265 to T.W. Higginson (7 June 1862)

ACKNOWLEDGMENTS

124. Gratitude grieves best. In letter 377 to Mrs. J.G. Holland (late August 1872)

ACKNOWLEDGMENTS

This story begins in sorrow and ends in blessing. So many people listened compassionately, I would need another book to thank everyone properly. With the humble word *thanks*, I acknowledge my debts to the following people.

Family members, who staggered with me through desolation and with whom I shared both loss and healing, thanked more fully below. Friends Susan Deborah (Sam) King and Susan Marie Swanson, whose friendship and wisdom helped steady me in the first few months. Maggie Swanson and Elaine Pagliaro, whose presence at the funeral and lifetime friendship is a treasure. Jim Gertmenian and others whose wise words are recorded in the pages of this book.

The members of the Minneapolis Churches Downtown Coalition for Grief Support, especially Mary Lou Carpenter, all of whom tenderly held my grief every Saturday for a year during the worst of it. New Jersey grief-support professionals for whose organizations I have volunteered and from whom I have learned so much, especially Joe Primo and Mary Fleck of Good Grief and Judy Pedersen of Interregnum/Hearts of Hope.

A village of writers and thinkers, friends and companions. Karen Thorkilsen and Sam King, whose close reading and patience with multiple, morphing drafts helped me shape this book into final form. Stephanie Hanson and Lisa Bullard, who read some of the very first chapters and gave me the beautiful compass that sits on my desk. Julie Maloney and members of the Women Reading Aloud work-in-progress group, whose observations helped to further clarify my thoughts. Members of the South Mountain Poets workshop, whose subtle insights helped me fine-tune some of the poems. Deborah Keenan, in whose Loft poetry workshops I first began to spread my wings. Elizabeth Ferry, Lyle Jenks, Dee Ready, Judy Christian, Diane Lynch, Heather Cook, Robin Whitely, Nathalie Bailey, and others who read slowly developing drafts and encouraged me. Eleanor Warnock, who thoroughly proofread the final manuscript. My sister, Mary Ann Ryan, who supported me from word one. Emily Blumenfeld and Nancy Gerber, my First Friday writers, who helped me stay faithful to this project. Susanna Rich, who entrusted her students to me as we explored Emily Dickinson and grief. Elizabeth Watson, Quaker writer and friend, whose grief memoir, *Guests of My Life*, was an early, indelible inspiration.

Kevin Atticks, Olivia Airhart, Mary Del Plato, Bennett Wisner, and everyone at Apprentice House Press for selecting *Grief's Compass*, taking on the challenges of its many voices, and bringing it into the world with such imagination.

Family, the bedrock of my life. My parents, Frances and Francis McKernon, of blessed memory; my mother-in-law, Susan Runkle, and father-in-law, of blessed memory, Bob Runkle; Laura and Paul Runkle and their families; all of you carried me in one way or another. My sister-in-law Madonna McKernon and children, models of courage and the power of love to nurture resilience. My sister, Mary Ann, and brothers Rob, Jim, Ralph, and Kevin, who suffered the loss of our brother and remain an integral part of this story. My husband, David, whose steadfast love is woven into my being, and our daughters, Anne and Sarah, whose lives are precious beyond measure; you three also suffered this loss, absorbed the depth of the shock, and walked the wilderness with me until I could say, with Emily Dickinson, "Gratitude grieves best."

Apprentice House is the country's only campus-based, student-staffed book publishing company. Directed by professors and industry professionals, it is a nonprofit activity of the Communication Department at Loyola University Maryland.

Using state-of-the-art technology and an experiential learning model of education, Apprentice House publishes books in untraditional ways. This dual responsibility as publishers and educators creates an unprecedented collaborative environment among faculty and students, while teaching tomorrow's editors, designers, and marketers.

Outside of class, progress on book projects is carried forth by the AH Book Publishing Club, a co-curricular campus organization supported by Loyola University Maryland's Office of Student Activities.

Eclectic and provocative, Apprentice House titles intend to entertain as well as spark dialogue on a variety of topics. Financial contributions to sustain the press's work are welcomed. Contributions are tax deductible to the fullest extent allowed by the IRS.

To learn more about Apprentice House books or to obtain submission guidelines, please visit www.apprenticehouse.com.

Apprentice House
Communication Department
Loyola University Maryland
4501 N. Charles Street
Baltimore, MD 21210
Ph: 410-617-5265 • Fax: 410-617-2198
info@apprenticehouse.com • www.apprenticehouse.com